Rambling On in the Northwest

John Singleton

Published by

MELROSE BOOKS

An Imprint of Melrose Press Limited
St Thomas Place, Ely
Cambridgeshire
CB7 4GG, UK
www.melrosebooks.com

FIRST EDITION

Copyright © John Singleton 2011

The Author asserts his moral right to
be identified as the author of this work

Cover designed by Hannah Belcher
Cover illustration by Ernie Ingham

ISBN 978 1 907040 90 0

Printed and bound in Great Britain by:
CPI Antony Rowe. Chippenham, Wiltshire

To everyone in the group…
For all the camaraderie and pleasure we have given
each other over the years.

Best Wishes

Mingleton

CONTENTS

Map of The Northwest			vi
Foreword			vii
Cartoon page of Characters			viii

WALKS

1.	Around Barley	'Witch Magic?'	1
2.	Boulder Valley – Levers Water	'Party Time'	21
3.	Levens Bridge – Sedgwick	'Plus One'	33
4.	Rufford	'The Big Sky'	49
5.	Entwistle	'Members Only'	61
6.	Hardcastle Crags	'Dogs Galore'	79
7.	Roeburndale	'Traumatic'	93
8.	Ings – School Knott	'Rainbows'	105
9.	Clapham – Crummackdale	'Pure Delight'	119
10.	Warton Crag	'Twice!'	131

About the Author		147

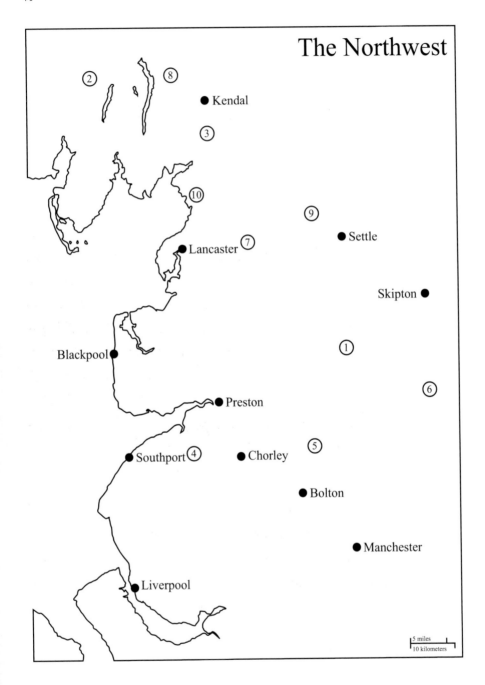

The Northwest

② ⑧

● Kendal

③

⑩

⑨

● Settle

Lancaster ⑦

Skipton ●

①

⑥

Blackpool ●

● Preston

Southport ④   ● Chorley   ⑤

● Bolton

● Manchester

● Liverpool

5 miles
10 kilometers

FOREWORD

All the characters are real, as indeed are the various incidents that arise during the walks. Although the book was never intended to be an out-and-out guide, it is nevertheless very adequate in this respect, especially when used in conjunction with the suggested OS maps and a little common sense. What I have tried to do is show that walking is fun and doesn't just depend on the walk itself. As you get a little older it is the company that matters, being able to laugh at and with each other, appreciate each other's difficulties, be able to rely on each other and yet be relaxed enough to enjoy all aspects of the walk to the full – no longer is it essential to claim this or that objective. A good walk for most people should be humanized and not necessarily a challenge.

I do hope that you enjoy these accounts of our rambles as much as I have enjoyed writing them and participating in them. Have a go… but be careful, wear suitable gear, take nourishment and drink with you, use the appropriate OS map, have basic first-aid materials, respect the countryside, but above all… enjoy yourselves.

Perhaps we'll meet up with you one day!

CHAPTER 1

AROUND BARLEY

'WITCH MAGIC?'

5 MILES

28 - 01 - 09

AROUND BARLEY

5 MILES (NB MAP NOT TO SCALE)

28 – 01 – 09

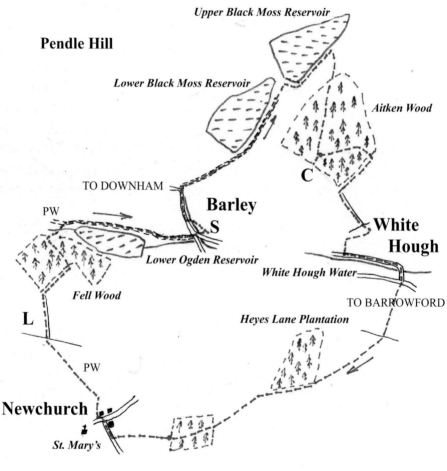

Pendle Hill

Upper Black Moss Reservoir

Lower Black Moss Reservoir

Aitken Wood

TO DOWNHAM →

C

PW

Barley

S

Lower Ogden Reservoir

→ **White**

Hough

White Hough Water

L

Fell Wood

TO BARROWFORD

Heyes Lane Plantation

PW

Newchurch

St. Mary's

TO FENCE AND A6068 AND M65

Map: *Ordnance Survey Explorer OL21 South Pennines*
Start: *GR 823404*

What a gloomy, grey morning! One of those mornings when, after peeping through the curtains, the idea of walking was rather ridiculous and a return to a somnolent posture for another hour or so was a much more attractive proposition. But being a member of a group has one major advantage – it makes you do things which you would normally have second thoughts about and often these 'enforced actions' are well rewarded, today being one of those fantastic days!

9.00 am and off we went into the mist with only a couple of hundred yards visibility; on the M6 it was no better, and the A59 along the Ribble Valley was even worse – no sign of anything except a short distance in front of the car. There was no sign of Pendle and its ridge or even the belching chimneys of the cement works at Clitheroe. We turned down to Chatburn, then on entering the beautiful village of Downham IT HAPPENED!! There was Pendle in all its glory, everywhere ahead was clear in every detail, you could see for miles – as good as I'd seen it. We pressed on along the Barley road rising steadily around the base of Pendle until we came to a stop at an advantageous position. Looking back across the Ribble Valley, we experienced an incredible sight – the length of the valley, from the west right up to Settle and Ingleborough, was full of a 'glacier' of dense mist, white and woolly but stationary – a truly magnificent natural phenomenon.

The Ribble Valley

*Ingleborough beyond
the misty valleys*

By the time we met up in the deserted car park at Barley everyone was excited about the now perfect conditions, the realization as to how lucky we were, and thankful that we had made it, thanks to each other. Walking! Bring it on!

Leaving the car park

The nine of us, plus our canine companions, left the northwest corner of the car park, crossed a footbridge and joined the main road to take us back through Barley. As the road turned sharp left at the edge of the village, we carried forward along a narrow walled lane which took us up to Lower Black Moss Reservoir. Here we came across another magical moment – the perfect reflection of the dominant Pendle and its surroundings in the reservoir's mirror-like surface.

Pendle reflects

Pendle and the reservoirs

On reaching the dam of the Upper Black Moss Reservoir we turned right and then, following the rough track round to the left, we walked along the reservoir until, part way along it, we turned right onto a concessionary path.

This forest road rose quite steeply diagonally across the hillside to gradually ease off as we entered Aitken Wood.

That's the worst over with!

That's better!

Ogden Valley

Rather than turn into Aitken Wood proper (narrow path on the left) we proceeded right, off the track, to the edge of the wood to partake of coffee. From our coffee perch on a pile of stones, we were afforded excellent views to the head of Ogden Valley in the west,

Coffee break

and to the south a moving, rolling mist rising out of the Calder Valley. Speaking of perches, throughout our break a 'thrush-like' bird, possibly a fieldfare, was sat in 'Christmas Fairy' pose on a nearby fir tree – another magical moment.

Southern mist

Top bird

I began to wonder whether all these 'different' sorts of experiences, albeit of the pleasant kind, were in some way to do with the fact that we were very much into WITCH country – Pendle and all that! Further evidence manifested itself as we backtracked to enter Aitken Wood. What an enchanting place it turned out to be as we headed down through the tall trees, which were separated by shafts of sunlight and yet held together by wisps of mist, rising out of an unusual undergrowth of small holly bushes.

Aitken Wood

Out of the wood

On leaving the wood a right turn, shortly followed by a left turn, took us down the side of a pasture which, just before we left it, reminded us of the recent heavy rainfalls. Having negotiated this muddy patch we then had to slip and slither down a steep bank before we reached a gravel path leading onto a narrow lane. By the side of the rough road flowed the river known as White Hough Water, which we now followed downstream to pass the rather opulent hamlet of White Hough on our left. This river is unusual in so far as it flows in a west to east direction before joining Pendle Water, another 'Water' river.

Muddy escape

Aitken Wood

White Hough Water

Weir below the bridge

Beyond the habitation, the road crossed over the river and then quickly ascended to the Barley-Barrowford road. This was crossed and the ascent continued more steeply up a pasture headland.

Another cardiovascular

From the justified rest point at the top of the slope a retrospective glance gave us excellent views inland to Stansfield Tower on Blacko Hill. Now the gradient decreased as, once through a stile incorporating an old stone gatepost, we headed along the narrow track towards Heys Lane Plantation.

Blacko Hill

Distant view of Stansfield Tower

Towards the wood

Old gatepost

The walk continued with a gentle rise by the left of the plantation to then ease left towards the centre of another small wood. Once into the wood and out of the sun the temperature dropped quite markedly and we were relieved when we emerged with the village of Newchurch in our sights. As we walked across the intervening field it was noticeable that the boundary houses had all been whitened – was this to do with the residents trying to counteract the rather grey 'witches' image perceived by most other people? But what's this? A black cat in our tracks – well, you can't have a more 'witchy' greeting than that! More magical moments?

Newchurch

Where's the broom? Sorry Val

Black magic!

Newchurch was one of the main players in the witchcraft persecution of the early 18th century in this part of the world. Superstition, vindictiveness, and panic together with the ruthless persecution of witches and Catholics by James I led to the trial and subsequent hanging of several local residents in 1612. Among these were Demdike and Chattox, two old women who most probably were delighted to be classed as unusual and hence to be feared by many, and Alice Nutter, a lady of substance and a landowner. Alice was also a devout Catholic and had just won a legal argument with Roger Nowell of Read Hall. Most probably these two factors, one bigoted, one of revenge, led to her death rather than classification as a witch – perhaps that is why her grave can be found in St Mary's Churchyard, Newchurch (close to the south side of the church).

And so we entered Newchurch along Jinny Lane to its junction with the Barley road by what used to be the Lamb Inn on the right and opposite the Witches Galore shop, another whitened establishment but, alas, today void of the 'three scarecrow-type witches' usually leaning against the wall – and so the dreadful happenings of yesteryear live on!

Newchurch

Witches Galore and the old Lamb Inn

Margaret and Val in situ – no further comment, please!

Above Newchurch

Our walk continued across the road to join up with the Pendle Way, a 45-mile circular path, opened in 1986, around the borough of Pendle. This took us by the left-hand side of the public toilets, along a narrow ginnel to quickly rise above the village and then head off, half left, towards a distant wall on the skyline. This part of the walk was very hard going, as the terrain was soggy and very uneven; it was indeed a relief when we finally made it to the wall and beyond the stile to the harder ground.

The long plod

Now the undulating path followed a wall to our right over which we had views of our coffee spot above Barley and forward, to the left, the solid lump of Pendle Hill. I wondered if the blemish to its left flank, looking like a landslide, was indeed the basis of the one mentioned in *The Lancashire Witches* by W. H. Ainsworth, a contemporary of Dickens.

Before going down to Fell Wood we decided to tarry awhile, with the pleasant sunshine on our backs, to enjoy lunch and the extensive northern views. Revitalized, we made our way down to the corner of the wood to then turn right over a stile (signposted to remind us that we were still on the Pendle Way) and followed the wide path down the side of the trees.

The Pendle Way

The odd fallen tree reminded us that, despite their height, the fir trees possessed a relatively shallow root structure – just how they remained upright in a gale is beyond me!

Root structure

Out of the wood

Once again, the drop in temperature as we entered the wood was quite amazing, it must have been several degrees, so much so that it was scarves etc. back on as we hurried our descent to the sunshine below – what a good decision it was to have had our lunch where we did. The steep path brought us out just above the Lower Ogden Reservoir where we used a typical Lancashire footbridge to cross the stream and join the waterworks road. Here we said goodbye to the PW as it turned left whilst we turned right to stride out along the good surface by the side of the reservoir.

Lower Ogden Reservoir

Down to Barley

Once we were level with the dam, the road dipped quite sharply only to level out as it passed the United Utilities filter station and then within minutes we were into Barley, only needing to cross the road to gain access to the car park. At this point, I would normally write about what a great day we had had, full of magical experiences and how we had all enjoyed it.

The car park

And so we had – absolutely marvellous – BUT it wasn't over yet! On our way home, in exactly the same place as we had seen it in the morning, we were presented with the river of white mist in the Ribble Valley – still magical, thank goodness for nature! As we eased up out of Downham to be enshrouded by the mist we thought of our day in 'Brigadoon', it will be a long time before we experience anything of that like again.

Still there!

A little smile of satisfaction and 'smug' thoughts did cross our minds --- how could we have been so lucky ? -- as we sped on into the murk of the A59.

I wonder if there are still witches about ? -- if so, on today's showing ,they must be very friendly ones.

CHAPTER 2

BOULDER VALLEY - LEVERS WATER

'PARTY TIME'

4+ MILES

04 - 09 - 07

BOULDER VALLEY - LEVERS WATER

4+ MILES (NB MAP NOT TO SCALE)

04 - 09 - 07

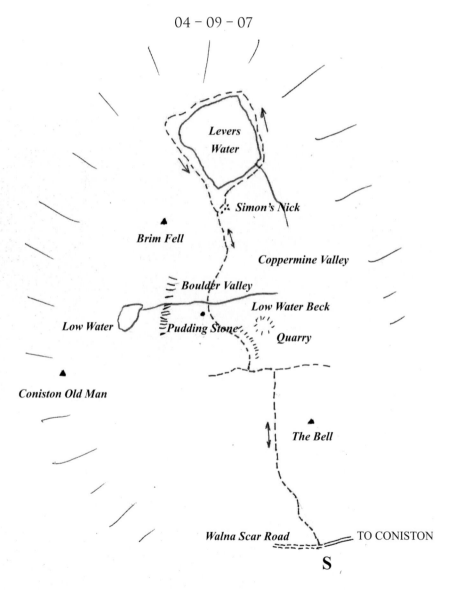

Map: *Ordnance Survey OL6 The English Lakes SW Area*

Start: *GR 288970*

A good turnout of ten members today and once again, despite the distance, all the cars arrived at the same time; in fact we actually followed each other up the steep narrow road out of Coniston to park on the rough ground at the start of the unsurfaced Walna Scar road. The weather was fantastic, blue sky with a few cotton-bud clouds, no wind yet just cool enough to make walking a delight – it augured well for a good day.

We headed north along the rough track, which was at right-angles to the Walna Scar road, towards the heart of the Coniston Group and the copper-mine area in particular.

Track heading north to the higher terrain

The track rose gently in snake-like fashion, passing The Bell, a rugged mass, to our right, until it reached the junction with the Coniston-Old Man path. We turned left along this main thoroughfare, but only for a short distance, before turning right onto a much narrower but still distinctive path.

The Bell

This high-level path, an old mining track, took us high above the quarries, clinging to the fellside as it made its way to overlook the entrance to the high-level Boulder Valley. This valley is really a natural shelf under the near-vertical 600 foot cliffs below Low Water. It is littered with fallen boulders, some of them being quite big, especially the one which we now reached. This was the 'Pudding Stone' a 25 foot high, as big as a house boulder, and it was by this natural monument that we partied.

Boulder Valley track

The Pudding Stone

Quarries below

Today 'Little Pete' reached that fine pecuniary age of 65 – it was something worth celebrating and I am sure a pleasant surprise for him. Miraculously from the depths of several rucksacks appeared a cake, a bottle of wine, paper plates, napkins, plastic glasses and goodness knows what else. The cake, Margaret's gluten-free sponge, was quickly creamed, Pete did  the necessary initial cut, pieces were passed round and, together with a glass of wine, everyone wished Pete a happy birthday with a resounding chorus of 'Happy Birthday to You'. Suddenly an echo was heard from across the nearby Low Water Beck as an unnoticed walking group enthusiastically joined in with another lusty rendition of the same. It was really a great moment. HAPPY BIRTHDAY PETE!!!

Party time

Rucksacks repacked, all litter collected, we crossed the beck, found our way through the many stacks of slabs and stones waiting to be used for some restructuring purpose (we'll most probably see the results next time we're in these parts) and headed up the nearly 'cardiovascular' path towards Simon's Nick, with its many old copper mine shafts, and thence to Levers Water. A couple of years ago as we walked this path in the opposite direction, the wind was so strong that we were sprayed by the waters of the beck and, I'm nearly sure, from Low Water itself, several hundred feet above us. The wind was so intense that the water cascading down out of Levers Water was blown back on itself, uphill! Whilst at the reservoir spirals of water several feet high issued from its turbulent surface. Today the waters were, like the day, peaceful and calm, full of reflections of its rugged, wild surroundings.

Boulder Valley

The path now led us past the fenced old copper mine shafts on our right and then down to the dam of Levers Water (Coniston's water supply), which we crossed to then follow the uneven path anticlockwise around this 'brooding' stretch of water.

Old copper mine shaft

On the dam

Around Levers Water

Just before completing the circumnavigation the path eased right to take us over the low shoulder of Brim Fell and back to the head of Boulder Valley. Now as we started to retrace our steps we could appreciate, on our descent, the views to our left, down onto the rather desolate legacy of the once prosperous (on and off since Roman times) Coppermine Valley and beyond to Coniston Water.

Coppermine Valley

Beyond Boulder Valley

After re-crossing Low Water Beck and admiring the Pudding Stone once more we left the confines of the Boulder Valley, the track taking us between newer looking spoil heaps that hadn't been noticed earlier, whilst below them a revitalized quarry indicated that all was not yet lost to nature in this area rich in industrial archaeology.

Out of Boulder Valley

The working quarry

All of a sudden we reached the Old Man path, it was like walking into another world – people galore – singles, groups, families, dogs – but it was good to see them all, without exception, enjoying themselves. Going along with much of the tide we made our way happily back to the vehicles, very contented after another excellent day in the Lakes and a party 't' boot'!!

Another wonder – no stiles nor gates. There aren't many walks like that!

Low Water Beck

CHAPTER 3

LEVENS BRIDGE - SEDGWICK

'PLUS ONE'

6 MILES

01 – 09 – 08

LEVENS BRIDGE - SEDGWICK

6 MILES (NB MAP NOT TO SCALE)

01 – 09 – 08

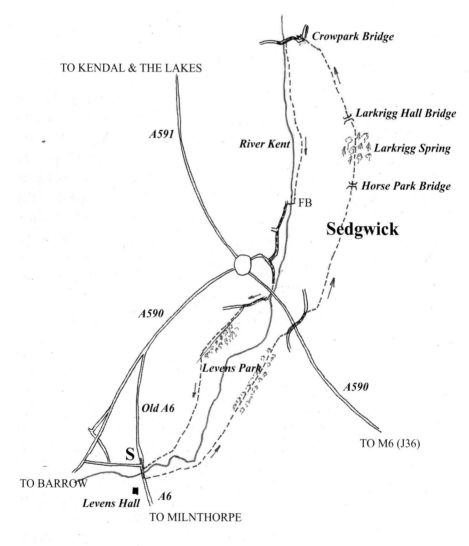

Crowpark Bridge

TO KENDAL & THE LAKES

Larkrigg Hall Bridge

A591

River Kent

Larkrigg Spring

Horse Park Bridge

FB

Sedgwick

A590

A590

Levens Park

TO M6 (J36)

Old A6

S

TO BARROW

Levens Hall

A6

TO MILNTHORPE

Map: Ordnance Survey OL7 The English Lakes – South East
Start: GR 496854

The day was rather gloomy as we assembled at the big lay-by on the old, one-way A6, close to its junction with the 'new' A6 at Levens Bridge north of Milnthorpe. Although the weather didn't look as though it was likely to improve, there was thankfully at present no precipitation and the atmosphere was one of buoyancy amongst the seven members and Thomas, our grandson, as we donned the necessary clobber for the occasion. And it was an occasion – the day being close enough to Ernie's birthday for us to celebrate it in a rather unique way.

As a group who have been together for a good number of years we have developed a number of mirthful topics concerning the individual which brings the 'worst!! (not really)' out of us at the expense of our fellow member – these feasts of merriment are always given and accepted in the best possible taste with a great feeling of lasting camaraderie. Today, the result of such spates of harmonious laughter saw the arrival of a small, curvaceous blonde joining us. She had been spotted by Margaret at a car-boot sale near Newark some weeks previously – the purchase was a hoot in itself, M being dropped like a lead balloon by her nearby family after disclosing the reason for the purchase to the stallholders and anyone else who would listen. Just before starting off, Margaret 'noticed!' that Ernie's rucksack was not as it should be and that if he'd just be still she would adjust it for him. As he stood patiently waiting for the necessary, she attached the lightweight 'blonde' to the rucksack of the unsuspecting Ernie. So off we went across the road with our little buxom member happily wobbling in tune with the gait of her new-found friend.

We followed the roadside path down to cross the River Kent and then immediately turned left to enter Levens Park. The park is separated from Levens Hall (renowned for its topiary and horse-drawn coaching events) by the A6 but it is still a place obviously proud of itself as it nurses the Kent until it ends on reaching the A590. It is full of fabulous trees: gigantic oak and beech, which for much of the way form a fantastic avenue of ancient natural monuments standing in resplendent verdant pasture grazed by endangered black and white Bagot goats and an unusual herd of black fallow deer. All this, together with glimpses of the meandering, sparkling necklace of the river, made it, despite the drab weather, an excellent start to the walk – and still we wobbled on!

The Kent

Bagot Goats

An enormous beech

Levens Park

Wobbling?

The avenue

Once through the park gates we turned left along the country lane to pass over the uncompromising A590 and then immediately right into a pastureland environment. We now quickly rose above the wooded valley of the Kent to join the intermittent bed of the northern end of the old Lancaster Canal, which in its 19th century heyday used to convey both goods and people between Kendal and Lancaster. Now all that remains of this once thriving thoroughfare are lone bridges in the middle of fields, short stretches of canal path, the occasional cutting full of trees and, as at Sedgwick, the remnants of an old quayside.

Kent Valley and A591

Canal path

Old canal bridge

Nevertheless we followed this 'canal' path for the next two miles of our walk and as we proceeded the weather slowly improved, so much so that on reaching the aqueduct at Sedgwick it became necessary to remove some of our outer garments!! Then is happened – the great kidology ended!

Much to Ernie's astonishment and our unrivalled mirth the new member slid from his rucksack to the ground and all was revealed. Ernie, as was expected, immediately joined in with the merriment and a good time was had by all – even Ginny appeared to look amazed at the maiden's appearance from on high then proceeded to wag her tail, enjoying the situation like the rest of us. Coffee was also appropriate at this moment of time.

Still wobbling

Hello! What's this?

However, thanks to Ernie's great sense of humour, our new friend was neither 'let down' nor abandoned; she was in fact reinstated onto her rucksack throne to enjoy the rest of the day with us.

The old aqueduct at Sedgwick

Sedgwick

Beyond Sedgwick, a village built on dynamite production, which used the canal to transport its wares down to the ports of Lancaster, Glasson and Preston for universal distribution, we continued along the line of the canal crossing farmland to reach the defunct Horse Park Bridge.

Horse Park Bridge

The path now passed through woodland at Larkrigg Spring where the canal was more obvious but trees and other vegetation occupied the well-defined canal floor. Once out of the wood, we were soon at Larkrigg Hall Bridge, not quite decommissioned as it is used as a crossover footpath and farm track. Interestingly on the bridge's stone uprights, because of the bend in the canal, could be discerned many grooves, caused over the years by the ropes used by the horses to drag the barges along.

Larkrigg Spring

Larkrigg Hall Bridge

Rope markings

Our canal trek terminated at the next bridge (Crowpark Bridge), this time a working
one, where we joined a country lane to head downhill towards the River Kent. Before
venturing along its eastern bank some of us had a look over the parapet of Hawes
Bridge in order to see the river as it plunged at breakneck speed through the gorge
below; surprisingly these rapids were being fished by a lone optimist.

From Hawes Bridge

We now headed south, downstream, along the river's eastern bank. Its turbulence
continued below us for a little way but soon gave way to a more leisurely pace, apart
from the white water caused by the occasional underlying bands of limestone – at one
of these we partook of lunch. The weather was good now as we relaxed in the sun,
enjoying our repast and the energetic displays of two white-breasted dippers as they
bobbed in and out of the water foraging between the rocks close to the opposite bank.

So on we went, following the Kent downstream, sometimes by its wide calm water, sometimes well above its turbulent raging mass, until we came upon a substantial metal suspension bridge – this was our crossing point of the river.

Lunch by the Kent

However, the bridge didn't appear quite as substantial as we had first thought, or at least it was not as rigid as we thought it might have been. Once on it the wobbling started, quickly reducing our confidence in it. Despite this there was always the temptation to encourage the swaying iron structure – to which some members succumbed!! I don't know what SHE, still perched on her throne, must have thought!

But on the other side SHE, once more, became the centre of attention as three women, waiting to cross in the opposite direction, were enthralled and puzzled by her appearance – this, amidst raucous laughter, was quickly explained. Each party departed in the best of spirits, having witnessed another triumph for colourful plastic.

We were now on a narrow road, which we followed up to another, then forward until at the next junction we turned left heading back down to the river. By a couple of houses we found the river in one of its energetic stages: rampaging, turbulent white water plunging down over a series of high rocky steps before passing under the nearby A590. At a vantage point overlooking the gardens we watched in amazement as time after time salmon attempted to leap over this 'boiling' water. Magnificent!! This was a first for most of us and it also helped to explain the fisherman we had seen earlier. Ironically, there was no sign of life on the salmon ladder immediately below us.

Sorry! There should have been a jumping salmon in the picture but somehow it got away!!

Perhaps my synchronization will improve in the future.

Fish ladder

The purpose-built pathway, high above the river, took us under the throbbing A590 to join a minor cul-de-sac lane rising away from the underpass.

A590 underpass

After a couple of hundred yards we turned left to walk over farmland before following a wall by the side of a wood until we came across a stile which allowed us to enter Levens Park once again.

I'm still with you

Levens Park

From our elevated position we began a long gentle saunter down through the park, not even disturbing a contented flock of sheep, until we eventually reached a large bend in the river and hence to the A6 and our waiting cars.

Our new member turned out to be very popular, so much so that she was invited to our Christmas dinner – well, we couldn't very well sit down with just thirteen members present!

CHAPTER 4

RUFFORD

'THE BIG SKY'

7 MILES

10 – 11 – 06

RUFFORD

7 MILES (NB MAP NOT TO SCALE)

10 – 11 – 06

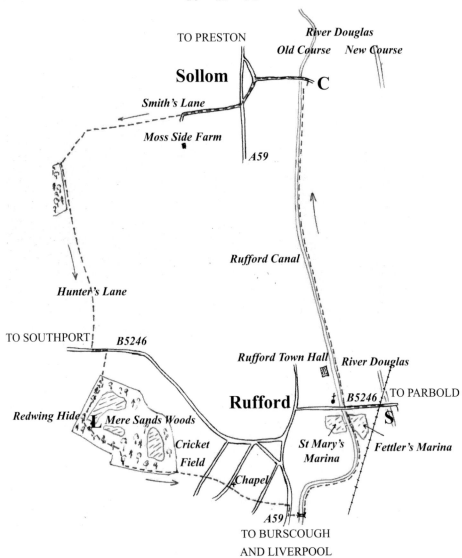

Map: Ordnance Survey Explorer 285 – Southport & Chorley

Start: GR 467156

It had been a shocker of a week! A typical November soul-destroying spell of greyness, interspersed with long spells of dampness, vanishing any belief that a sun still existed and that daylight should follow night. At least the decision to abandon the original destination and opt for a local venue was easily made. Optimistically we hoped for the best as we pessimistically donned our array of waterproofs at the Rufford station car park. It was just, but only just, raining as we crossed over the railway to follow the road to the canal.

Rufford station

The road passes between Fettlers Wharf, a marina, on the left and Alsley Lodge, an old folks' home, on the right. As both were initiated by the same person I presume that the former was named after the beer which was brewed during the Home's previous use, as the Fermor Arms pub. The word 'fettler' is a locally used term meaning friend as in 'now me ol' fettler, 'ow yer doing?' Incidentally the imposing building which the single-storey pub replaced (also called the Fermor Arms) had to be demolished when it started to subside on its foundations of cotton bales!

At the bridge, we turned right onto the towpath and headed northwards in the direction of Tarleton. The Rufford Canal is the northerly spur of the Leeds and Liverpool Canal, linking it to the Douglas Estuary, hence the River Ribble, and quite recently to the Lancaster Canal north of the Ribble. The part of the canal which we were now walking dates from 1760, as it was once part of the Douglas Navigation, linking the sea with Wigan and its coal mines. The canalized Douglas was replaced by the Rufford Canal when the spur was finished in 1781 but our present section survived as the northern section.

We were soon walking adjacent to the half-timbered Ruffold Old Hall, a National Trust property, built in the early 15th century by Sir Thomas Hesketh. A visit is to be recommended.

Ruffold Old Hall

As we emerged from the overhanging trees we were miraculously greeted with blue sky; was this to be our lucky day?

Rufford Canal

The towpath was several feet above the surrounding ground, subsequent drainage since the 18th century having caused the land to sink from its level inauguration days. We were soon at the old Sollom Lock where the man-made canal merged into the old course of the River Douglas (man-adapted for canal use). The present river flows between its straight constructed banks a couple of hundred yards to the east.

Sollom Lock – coffee time

The old Douglas Rufford Canal, north of Sollom Lock

Sitting on the round bench by the bridge, we enjoyed our coffee still unable to believe our luck with the weather. We crossed over the canal and at the road junction, in the small hamlet of Sollom, we turned left along the old winding Liverpool-Preston 'highway' to join the modern A59 within a short distance.

Hungry observers on our approach to the A59

Alas, the beautiful blue skies were once more beginning to give way to dark, heavy-looking ones as we negotiated the main road and headed off along a narrow tarmac farm road known as Smith's Lane onto the flat, fertile mosslands of West Lancashire.

Smith's Lane

The 'big sky' was both angry and beautiful as it sought its revenge on us for even considering to venture forth across these open mosslands, and would surely teach us a lesson before long. This must have been a stark contrast for two of our party, B & T, who had just returned from a holiday in Egypt!

Threatening

As the tarmac road swung left towards Moss Side Farm, we carried forward, following a cart track along the edge of a field and then at a junction of tracks we took a slight turn to the left by a line of trees in the direction of woodland, the profile of which merged ominously with the backdrop of the heavy black clouds.

Onto the cart track

On reaching the corner of the wood, surprise! Surprise! We got wet; the bigger surprise was that it didn't last long. We now turned left along a substantial cart track (Hunter's Lane) to head south across another swathe of mossland. From time to time we came across small sections 'paved' with big cobbles – perhaps this had been more than just a cart track a number of years ago, even linking the villages on the edge of this once swampy area. Later, after speaking to a local farmer, we learned that the more probable reason for these stones was to combat the wet and sinky parts on the mossland. Avoiding the many puddles, some of which were pond size, the lane eventually brought us out onto the B5246, the Rufford-Holmeswood road.

Mossland

The line of trees

Hunter's Lane

Another 'shower' joined us as we turned left for a short distance along the road but, as we turned right towards Mere Sands Wood, the rain must have continued forward towards Rufford. We were soon into the delightful environs of this Lancashire Wildlife Trust project, a strongly recommended venue for nature lovers, twitchers and woodland amblers alike. The excellent path took us in an anticlockwise direction around the periphery of the woods until at the 'Redwing' hide in its southwest corner we encamped in order to enjoy the huge lake and its inhabitants as well as to eat our lunch in guaranteed dry conditions.

The lake from the hide

Once again the gods were with us; as we dined, bright blue skies gradually pushed away the stormy clouds of the morning. Whilst we were using the hide for our unorthodox needs we were disturbed by the local newly formed U3A walking group which we had seen earlier out on the moss; I don't know who were the most surprised! On leaving the hide it was like walking into another world, we were into a beautiful spring-like day. Yes indeed, this was our lucky day! We now proceeded with a much lighter step, following the path along the southern borders of the wood bedecked in its late autumn costume sparkling in the low November sunshine. As we approached an estate we left this delightful setting but retained our proximity with the brook which had been our companion for the previous couple of hundred yards. We followed it upstream past the local cricket field and then onwards, crossing three metalled roads in the process, until, after passing a scrapyard, we emerged onto the A59. Considering the low and level terrain which we had been crossing, the stream had flowed with an inexplicably great haste – a puzzlement or optical illusion! Most probably neither, as the stream was heading for the very deep cut, Rufford Boundary Sluice, which we had previously followed along the southern edge of the wood.

Redwing hide

Mere Sands Wood

Along the southern edge of Mere Sands Wood

Rufford cricket field

Old chapel at the second road

We turned right along the busy road, but only for a short distance, thank goodness! At this point the road and canal were within spitting distance of each other so we crossed them both to then turn left along the 'greensward' towpath in the direction of Rufford. The towpath passed between two large marinas, the left one being St Mary's Wharf whilst the near one was the Fettler's Wharf which we had passed at the outset. The marinas are a recent addition to the delights of the canal; both, most probably, anticipating the increase in canal traffic now that the southern end of the Lancaster Canal has been linked, via the Ribble, to this one – very entrepreneurial!

The 'big sky' on this lowland walk had been a vast canvas for that wonderful accompanying artist, Nature, to display all its diverse talents – fantastic!

Fettler's Wharf

CHAPTER 5

ENTWISTLE

'MEMBERS ONLY'

5.5 MILES

01 − 04 − 09

ENTWISTLE

5.5 MILES (NB MAP NOT TO SCALE)

01 – 04 – 09

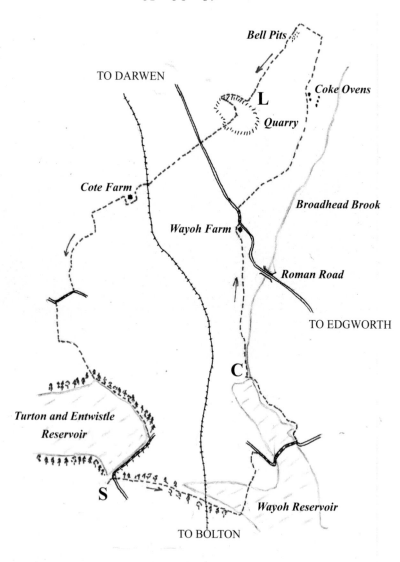

Bell Pits

TO DARWEN

Coke Ovens

L

Quarry

Cote Farm

Broadhead Brook

Wayoh Farm

Roman Road

TO EDGWORTH

C

Turton and Entwistle
Reservoir

Wayoh Reservoir

S

TO BOLTON

Map: *Ordnance Survey Explorer 287 – West Pennine Moors*

Start: *GR 722173*

April 1st – April Fools' Day – and the date was never mentioned!! But what a scenario – two cars, two car parks, each reached by separate roads and yet only a matter of one hundred or so yards apart. After twenty minutes of waiting for each other, slowly a realization materialized and with a walk up the steps a meeting was achieved and within minutes the cars were united on the top car park. Still no reference to the date, unbelievable!!

Reunited we were, but unfortunately in the wrong car park!! Our path started off from the lower car park (still no reference to April 1st). However, once we had found our way out of the parking area the day improved; in fact, the walk was first class as you will no doubt realize if you read on.

On our way at last!!

Wayoh Reservoir

So on we went along the concessionary path, looking down onto the narrow westerly arm of Wayoh Reservoir, until we turned left to cross the arm by means of a narrow causeway. Above us to our left, a train on the Bolton-Blackburn line crossed the multi-arched viaduct; what a view the passengers must have had looking over us down the length of the reservoir!! A lone grebe, quite undisturbed by our incessant chatter, repeatedly dived into the dark water as we made our way along the causeway.

Railway viaduct

Lonely grebe

Wayoh Reservoir looking towards Edgworth

Away from the reservoir

At the end of the causeway we followed a sunken track climbing to a path junction where we turned right towards a residency and hence onto a narrow metalled road. The roadway quickly descended round a hairpin bend, down to another causeway.

The start of this causeway across the eastern arm of the same reservoir was marked by a charismatic beech tree doing its best to awake from its winter slumbers, garlanded by an array of daffodils and, once again, as we crossed the causeway, we were treated to more nearby feathered friends, this time a group of Canada geese.

The beech tree

The second causeway

At the end of the causeway, we turned left to follow the path along the side of the reservoir, heading towards its most northerly point. As we proceeded, a lonesome toad jumped across our path causing us to once more enjoy and appreciate the presence of nature on our walks.

A left turn

Along the reservoir

When we arrived at the head of Wayoh Reservoir, suitable seating places reminded us that coffee was due. Within minutes of settling down to our beverage we were disturbed by movement in the nearby short grass. Instantly we became ultra-interested observers of nature's ultimate act – that of procreation, well, at least the first part of such a ritual. Two small male frogs were in deep conflict, each being interested in the nearby much larger female trying to make her way to the nearby water. Each male was intent on being with her when she would reach this point, full well knowing that their own contribution would then be required. The battle raged on for several minutes before Val and Margaret finally gave all of them a hand to achieve their goal by carrying them over to the water – we do see some things!!

We had thought that we had got the excitement of viewing 'nature in the raw' out of our systems but there was more evidence of this 'courtship' going on in the water as we progressed upstream along the man-enhanced Broadhead Brook, a feeder to the reservoir. The stream at first had a canalized appearance with a cobbled bed, whilst further upstream the sharp meanderings were strengthened by vertical stone flags. As we rose towards Wayoh Farm we looked up the deep valley to see the road bridge which dates back to Roman times – this was the route taken by the Romans to link Manchester (Mamucium) to Ribchester (Bremettanacum), their crossing point of the River Ribble, in the north.

Broadhead Brook

Roman road and bridge

Wayoh Farm

Now I'm not sure just where or why it started, whether it was because of the 'frog' episode or as a result of a conversational topic concerning the misuse and abuse of the English language, but from here on in the word 'member' became the word of the day. In its many guises it gave rise to much merriment, pretended disgust, innuendo after innuendo, innocent but funny remarks (see subtitle) – perhaps to the reader it doesn't say much about us as a group but, believe you me, we enjoy ourselves and each other's company, knowing full well how every one of us will respond. In fact, it actually showed me just how naïve I was, as I'd never heard this word being used in this correct context, having originally thought that this was a further abuse of our language.

Having passed through the yard of the opulent 'farm' property, we joined the 'Roman' road on a bend (where did they go wrong?). We followed this to the left for a short distance before turning right onto a farm track which we gradually ascended until at a junction we eased left, still rising, along what was now a rough track.

As the track took us out onto the moor above the deep valley of the aforementioned brook, ahead of us several black splodges appeared, a group to our right and one adjacent to the path ahead. These gradually changed into what looked like black, old-fashioned beehives; they were in fact old coke ovens where the poor coal from the nearby 'bell-pits' was converted into coke before being transported for industrial use in the surrounding towns. On closer inspection there was much evidence, both around and inside the ovens, to show their use many years previously.

The old coke ovens
High above the deep Broadhead Brook Valley

A short distance beyond the upper coke ovens we turned left to follow the remnants of an old wall onto the open moorland. This proved to be rather heavy going until we reached a cross wall close to a series of bell-pits, a source of the previously mentioned coal.

Across the moor

The old bell-pits

A move for a short distance left along the wall brought us to a gap which we passed through. Then, turning half left in a southwest direction, we crossed rough upland pasture (easy walking) to the edge of an enormous quarry. Here, on its lip, we lunched – and the 'conversation' continued!!

Towards the quarry

The huge quarry

Speculation as to when the quarry was last worked, what the stone was used for and how it had been transported away (from this position there was no obvious entrance through the vertical walls) also entered our conversation, thereby lifting it to a much higher intellectual level!!

On closer scrutiny from our perch, there did appear to be, on the western fringe, a way down to the floor of the quarry; this was the way we proceeded after lunch. The difficult descent took us into this stone industrial cathedral of yesteryear. It must, at one time, have swarmed with men and machinery as the stone was hewn out to be used in the industrial townships of East Lancashire. Now it looked rather sad with its stone pillars, rusty machinery, black quarry pools and deserted blasted rock – perhaps the ultimate in stone epitaphs, a veritable *Marie Celeste*.

However, nature was gradually beginning to heal this necessary man-made scar on the landscape but the process is slow in this barren environment and most probably it will always remain a legacy to man's ingenuity. I hope that it does and resists the present upward trend in the value of large holes! By following the path to the right across the quarry, we discovered the very narrow entrance to the complex. A well-disguised diagonal cutting through its southwest face took us onto a wide, well-defined, walled track leading straight down to and across the 'Roman' road previously encountered.

Quarry entrance

The walled track

The 'Roman' road

Beyond the road, the track continued unerringly in a straight line down to the railway. I would guess that this had once been the old truck line carrying the stone down to the railway for distribution. At the railway line, the track terminated in a small copse situation, which had most probably covered what had once been the areas that were used for the end-products from the quarry. This area, along with the widening of the railway track at this point, probably for sidings, could be seen more clearly as we crossed the line by means of the metalled footbridge.

The truck road

The copse area etc. from the footbridge

Entrance

Quarry

Truck Road

Copse

Railway

Looking back

The path, now enclosed, ascended the steep banking to Cote Farm and continued clockwise around the property before releasing us onto a wider track, still rising, across poor pastureland. When opposite a nearby farmstead to our right we turned sharp left and then at the next stile eased right along the man-made 'ditch' (or sunken track) which curved left in a wide arc before straightening to join a narrow metalled road.

The ditch?

A short stroll to the right along the road brought us to a sharp right turn; here we turned left to descend along a tree-lined sunken road.

The sunken road

This leafy road terminated at a small plateau with views through the trees down to the Turton and Entwistle Reservoir, but we didn't tarry; instead we turned left to walk along a level grassy 'ledge' to the edge of the wood. Here a further autumnal slope took us down to the castellated wall of the reservoir where with a left turn we stepped out to follow the roadway along its eastern shore.

Grassy ledge

The final leafy slope

I am pretty sure that our route from the quarry to this point had, at one time, something to do with the transport of the stone for its use in the building of the reservoir and its surrounds.

Turton and Entwistle Reservoir

By this time our conversational piece had subsided but it was momentarily revitalized as we turned right onto the dam and read the fishing notice!! What a laugh we had!! This enjoyment prevailed as we crossed the dam and back up to our vehicles.

Not only had we dealt with the vagaries of the English language, beheld nature in the raw, wondered as to our forefathers' industrial ingenuities and achievements, walked ancient roadways, survived the folklore of April 1st, but, on a more personal note, Margaret and I had thoroughly enjoyed this, the last walk, before our Golden Wedding on the 4th. It had indeed been a first-class walk!!

Margaret and myself

CHAPTER 6

HARDCASTLE CRAGS

'DOGS GALORE'

5.5 MILES

17 – 08 – 09

HARDCASTLE CRAGS

5.5 MILES (NB MAP NOT TO SCALE)

17 – 08 – 09

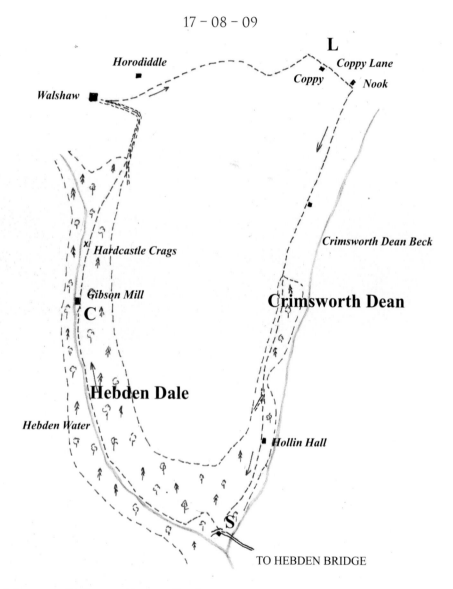

Map: *Ordnance Survey Explorer OL21 – South Pennines*

Start: *GR 989 292*

Having negotiated 'car-wash' conditions on our way we eventually all duly assembled on the National Trust car park (all paid-up members) at Midgehole (off the A6033 Keighley road just north of Hebden Bridge). Before the engine had cooled, a saturated couple and their equally wet but very friendly dogs arrived back at their adjacent car and then within seconds of their departure a group of excited dogs fell out of another vehicle and bounded around enjoying their freedom, nearly knocking young Alex over in the process. Was this to be a doggy day? In actual fact, little did we know that we would encounter this friendly pack later, as they made off under the direction of their lady minder. The weather was still threatening as we donned our protective gear, and the future didn't look at all inviting as the ten of us and our lone canine representative, Poppy Collins, started the walk.

Nearly ready

A right turn out of the car park past the old lodge, quickly followed by a left one, and we were soon down to the banks of the swift-flowing Hebden Water. We now followed this riverside path and its sylvan environment upstream for the next mile and a half as far as Gibson Mill.

Riverside path

This popular path in the deep-cut valley of Hebden Dale follows as close to the babbling beck as safety will allow. Sometimes only within earshot of the beck it wanders through the trees, entangled in their root systems, whilst, at others, over rocks within splashing distance of the energetic waterway. Along with man-made steps and the odd set of robust stepping-stones this was a most interesting path with which to explore the valley floor but it also demanded a fair amount of concentration, especially in the wet conditions which we were now experiencing.

Hebden Dale
Riverside path

This enjoyable but extremely 'damp' walk was somewhat diminished when we came across our earlier-met friendly pack still prancing about quite happily whilst their handler was being berated by a hysterical woman obviously distraught by the presence of the dogs. But instead of quickly moving away with her embarrassed companion she continued to verbally abuse the elderly woman, who remained quiet and calm. By using her phone as a camera (for evidence!) and ringing the police for assistance – how ridiculous can you get!! – the younger agitator continued to aggravate the dodgy situation. As a group, we moved between the antagonists without the slightest bother as the friendly pack moved around quite oblivious to the predicament of their handler. We did however hang about until the neurotic female was finally persuaded to move on, still squealing uncontrollable threats at the poor woman. We finally left the dog walker (that's what she appeared to be) composing herself although I must say that she looked quite unfazed by the incident, as though it wasn't the first time – perhaps, in hindsight, she should have shown a little more control over her dogs. On reflection, this incident most probably enhanced our walk as it distracted us from the sorry situation of our own rapidly increasing drenched conditions.

Gibson Mill

Nevertheless we pressed on, passing a small ideal picnic area by a set of stepping-stones, before arriving at the imposing Gibson Mill – and then we noticed that the precipitation had actually stopped!!

Gibson Mill, an old water-powered cotton mill founded in 1800, lasted less than a century before closing in 1892. Since then it has had a varied history including being a dance hall and later a roller-skating rink. Recently, as a National Trust property, it has been revamped as a museum and tearooms together with the usual facilities suitable for the many walkers and seasonal visitors to the area.

We used these facilities to good effect, casting off our now defunct waterproofs, allowing ourselves to dry off, and enjoyed our coffee using the picnic tables provided.

Now, with our spirits on the rise, as the sun pushed through the clouds, we made our way onto the Mill's rough access road, passing the mirror-like millpond to start a steady climb towards the head of the valley. Still surrounded by trees we soon passed the well-known and much-visited Hardcastle Crags, although with either heads bent downwards or deep in conversation, many of our group missed the titled objective of our walk. Not to worry, perhaps the enclosed photo will suffice!

Gibson Mill

Away from the mill

Hardcastle Crags

As the rough access road took us up and out of woodland it merged with another, more substantial one, from the right. Across to our left, dominating the head of the valley, was the old shooting lodge at Walshaw, a small farming community serviced by the access road we were now following. Having finally readjusted our apparel we moved on towards Walshaw (passing still more heavily cropping rowan trees), but just before entering the hamlet we turned tight right along a walled track.

Junction of access road

Walshaw

Shooting Lodge

Pete (grandad) and Alex

Another delightful rowan tree

The track soon opened up and headed out across pastureland, beneath the sturdy-looking property of Horodiddle, towards a wall. We now followed this rising wall as it arced its way up the side of the grazing land until at the top of the ascent the path suddenly passed through the wall and out on to open moorland.

Walshaw

Horodiddle

What a contrast! The mid-green of the pasture fringed with the dark green of the woodland below and now into the beiges of the moorland intermingled with patches of purple heather. Well worth seeing and what a wall separating them! Made up of flat stones, similar to small flags, topped by evil-looking vertical pieces of the same material – very substantial.

The rough track kept with the wall as it swung anticlockwise round the foot of Shackleton Knoll until, at a gate, we turned right where the track became enclosed. This was Coppy Lane, which originated as part of a 17th century trading route between Lancashire and the Calder Valley. Part way down the lane we came across Coppy, an old farmstead now in ruins, where, overlooking Upper Crimsworth Dean, we reclined and enjoyed our lunch.

Coppy

Just as we were restarting our descent a large greyhound bounded by with its two young owners in tow but, alas, they were gone before Poppy could enjoy their company – a likely story!

Coppy Lane

At the bottom of Coppy Lane, by another ruin (Nook), a right turn took us down an improved track high above Crimsworth Dean Beck in the deep valley below. As we walked and noisily talked on the gradual descent, at the first habitation we were accosted by a startled, mongrelized Labrador which aggressively bounded out at us; but, startled once again, it beat a hasty retreat as our little canine companion this time took charge of the situation.

The access road soon entered the confines of the woods of Crimsworth Dean, although from time to time it crossed an open expanse exposing an old quarry and enclosed grazed pasture acreage.

Nook

Access road

Valley of Crimsworth Dean Beck

To the woods

The now solid road took us steadily downhill, easing left at a Y junction and passing Hollin Hall, also on the left, until, after passing through the public car park at Midgehole, we finally made it back to our vehicles.

Varying weather, changing scenery, doggy interludes and Pete's rowan trees!! You never get bored on our walks!! A good day after a very wet start.

CHAPTER 7

ROEBURNDALE

'TRAUMATIC'

6.5 MILES

27 – 10 – 09

ROEBURNDALE

6.5 MILES (NB MAP NOT TO SCALE)

27 – 10 – 09

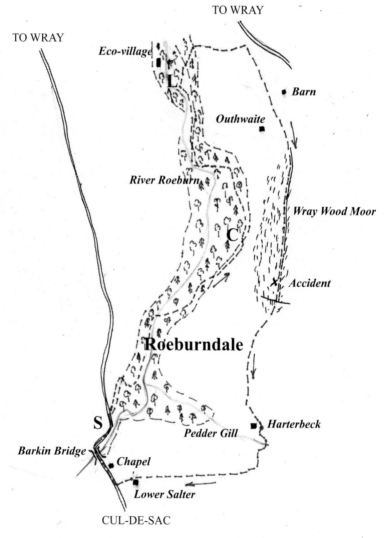

Map: *Ordnance Survey Explorer OL41 – Forest of Bowland*

Start: *GR 601638*

This was meant to be a walk to appreciate the delights of autumnal tints as displayed by the woods of mid-Roeburndale, facilitated by the use of a seldom walked concessionary path. This part of the walk was actually achieved but the return journey across the inhospitable Wray Wood Moor proved to be far more traumatic! But more of that later. In fact even before assembling at Barkin Bridge we experienced a minor trauma in the Lancaster area of our journey north – the northbound slip road off the M6 at Lancaster, our exit, was closed. Because of early warnings we came off at Hampson Green to eventually end up in the gridlock through the centre of Lancaster – oh dear!! – patience, boy, patience!! We were the last to arrive at the designated Barkin Bridge towards the top end of the deep Roeburndale Valley due south of the village of Wray, some ten miles east of Lancaster. Having told of our woes it turned out that ours had been the worst decision. Pete had had Geoff to guide him through the lesser known parts of the city whilst Jack went up to Carnforth before driving back across the Lune without any hold-ups.

It was time to be off, so we back-tracked a few yards to the A-stile on our right, the start of the concessionary path which would take us over two miles on a wandering journey through and round the dense woodland to the Middlewood footbridge. The path proved to be rather ill-marked and very indistinct in places. Still, with alert observation and commonsense we rose to the occasion and began to enjoy what we had come to see – autumn in its multi-coloured coat.

A stile

The start

Into the valley

For the first part of the walk the path took us above the wood but, once entered, the steep path dropped through the trees to the valley floor where the River Roeburn gurgled merrily along its rocky bed. A little downstream, we crossed a footbridge to then climb up through the forest, leaving the river way below us and out of sight. Now the path, what we could see of it, wandered in the upper echelons of the wood, occasionally leaving it, but only following its border, before once more diving into the safety of the sylvan world. At our last re-entry we had our coffee.

River Roeburn

Coffee time

The woods of Roeburndale

We now maintained our height as we progressed through the trees, doing our best not to be enticed into a premature descent (the valley side was very steep and therefore a potential hazard). A more obvious path was reached as we did, at last, start our descent.

At a clear junction, we eased left to follow the path which clung to the edge of a precipitous drop down to the Roeburn below. We were however soon down to the side of the river where some camping and minor logging activity had recently taken place.

From what I can gather this was linked to the Middlewood Community Ecovillage based further downstream and also to a camping barn, accessed over a dodgy-looking swing bridge to our left.

Quite a drop!

Apparently the barn, and also from time to time the 'yurts' which are normally lived in by the commune members, are available for hire by the public. A few years ago we approached this encampment, perched on a high banking overlooking the river further downstream, from the other side – it struck us as being a shambolic, quirky, idle way of escapist living. However, since acquiring its Ecological Trust status it appears to have taken on a more organized, and I suppose a more useful, purpose in this present 'green' age.

Now on level ground, what a relief, we headed downstream in the direction of the Eco village across a couple of meadows, following the much broadened river until, at a rather questionable ford, we camped down on the bank to enjoy our lunch.

I must emphasize that the morning's walk had been beautiful, the autumnal tints glorious – they had not disappointed! However, for anyone undertaking this section of the walk along the concessionary path I must point out that it is not an easy one to follow and great care should be taken.

Luncheon spot

Relaxed on the banks of the bubbly Roeburn, it was hard to realize that this river had caused such havoc and devastation in the village of Wray in 1967. In August of that year, the intake area of the Roeburn was subject to a phenomenal cloudburst causing a downpour of an average three inches in two hours, although a maximum of 4.6 inches was recorded in ninety minutes. This flash flood manifested itself in the village, destroying three houses and two bridges, causing ten further houses to be demolished in the aftermath but, thank goodness, with no loss of life.

We moved on to soon join a cross track which, to the left, would have taken us over the footbridge to the village, but instead we turned right to then head left, diagonally up the side of the valley. The path took us out of the wood and onto open pastureland, which we now crossed slightly to the right. After a further two fields, now close to a country lane, we turned right to pass through a squeeze-stile in a short stone wall. A steady upward trudge followed, keeping by the right-hand hedge side, passing a lone barn, until the access drive of Outhwaite, a moorland farm, was reached.

Looking back to the wood

The lone barn

Outhwaite

The roadway was crossed and the wall, now on our left, was followed over the next pasture. What a change beyond the next stone stile!! A rushy, marshy, moorland wilderness – utterly desolate save for the odd sheep and the dissecting walls, which stood out in the hostile beige terrain. At least they were a welcome sight, as we had to follow the main wall on our left for the next couple of miles in order to negotiate this morass known as Wray Wood Moor.

Wray Wood Moor – just before it happened!

Part-way along, this wall appeared to vanish but on reaching the spot it could be seen that it had actually been demolished (for what reason 'tis hard to comprehend) with the stones spread out close to their original position – at least, with care, we could still follow it. Over the next stile, we crossed a shallow brook and some wetter ground, causing the party to spread out rather more than usual. TRAUMA!!! From the rear a loud, sharp, anxious cry was heard followed by further cries for assistance. Looking round, a quick response found us running back (often staggering) towards the huddle of people around the now prostrate body of my MARGARET!! It was her left arm lying in a peculiar position which was the cause of concern. There was no bleeding but it was so obviously broken, just above the wrist. No good looking at it – into the rucksack – primitive the first-aid kit might have been but wasn't I glad that Margaret had insisted that we carry it – Margaret's ashen face telling us of the pain she was in – bandage to bind the break securely and as a support – a triangular cloth for a sling – already a look of determination was returning to her face – what next? – A quick assessment – two miles or so back to the car, nearest habitation with access? – Back to Outhwaite or forward to Harterbeck? (Neither would be easy) – Forward the best bet? – Was Margaret up to it? – I thought so and she certainly did as the adrenaline was starting to take over.

Margaret had apparently stood on a wobbly submerged stone, put out her arm to break the fall, this had landed on another, this time more solid, stone under the water and the accident was complete. It was most fortunate that the skin had not been broken as the water was in a sad state of purity – be thankful for small mercies in an emergency!

Off we go!

There was no time to waste; the walk, as a walk, was abandoned, everyone volunteering to help in any way that seemed appropriate. Our progress did not slow as we continued over the last piece of inhospitable terrain and over a wooden A-stile (great care here) and out onto easier pastureland. Margaret was fantastic, as the adrenaline really kicked in, striding out with that recognizable look which I have known over the years – a mixture of stubbornness and determination showing great willpower but always with a smile on her face despite the ordeal.

Out of Pedder Gill gully

As we approached the farmstead of Harterbeck I knew that now she was on the go, she would insist on going all the way back to the car, and so it proved. Leaving the farm, the trek was rather dodgy, especially in the descent to cross Pedder Gill (neither the time nor the inclination to view the gorge and the falls) and then up the steep banking on the other side.

Now we were above the deep gully the tension gradually decreased as the worst was over; it was downhill all the way back to the car. The path, though rather wet underfoot, eased right to head down to the farmstead of Lower Salter.

Down to Lower Salter

The delight and relief on everybody's faces as our feet hit the solid driveway of the farm was great to see; personally it was like a great weight being taken off my shoulders. Margaret was still in fine spirits as we passed the small chapel on our way down to the cars beyond Barkin Bridge.

Solid!

Lower Salter Chapel

Barkin Bridge

WE'D MADE IT!! What a relief! But we hadn't finished yet as we made a quick exit from the pull-in parking area. With Margaret as comfortable as possible we decided to bomb down the motorway to deal with her problem on home territory. She entered the A&E at Chorley Hospital at 5.30 pm and arrived home 'well casted' by 7.00 pm. JOB DONE!!

Possibly a day to remember but I hope never to be repeated. On reflection, this day and the walk itself had had, certainly for me personally, very few relaxing moments – I doubt that we, Margaret and I, will venture into these parts again. However, we as a group have always maintained that there are positives in every walk and to be truthful, this was no exception – the autumnal colours amidst the superb trees, the deer bounding away in front of us but above all the camaraderie displayed within our group.

Margaret and I are very grateful for all your help and co-operation,
MANY, MANY THANKS.

P.S. Margaret was successfully discharged from Chorley Hospital on Tuesday 29th December; nine weeks to the hour after having suffered a bad fracture and dislocation of her lower ulna.

CHAPTER 8

INGS - SCHOOL KNOTT

'RAINBOWS'

5 MILES

17 – 11 – 09

INGS - SCHOOL KNOTT

5 MILES (NB MAP NOT TO SCALE)

17 - 11 - 09

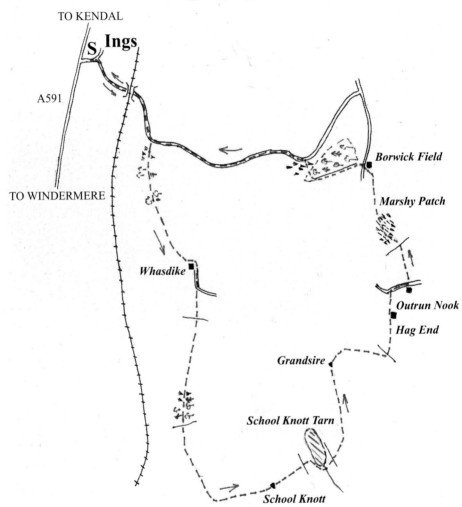

TO KENDAL

S **Ings**

A591

TO WINDERMERE

Borwick Field

Marshy Patch

Whasdike

Outrun Nook

Hag End

Grandsire

School Knott Tarn

School Knott

Map: *Ordnance Survey Explorer OL7 – English Lakes SE Area*

Start: *GR 445987*

Should we? Shouldn't we? It had been that sort of a week, especially in the last few days when we had had lots of rain with much more pending. Nevertheless, as there appeared to be a slight window of reasonable weather imminent, we decided to give it a go, and fortunately were subsequently rewarded for our temerity.

Six of us joined forces on the small car park at the end of the lane going through the village of Ings just as it rejoins the A591 northwards. A few sharp blue patches were present in the rather angry turbulent sky – had we made the correct decision? – as we walked away from the major road to turn immediately right along a narrow country lane.

Rainbow 1

Railway ahead

To the north, a fine rainbow watched our progress along the lane as it took us under the railway to then rise steeply for a short distance where, as it levelled out, at a sharp left bend we parted company, to cross some ominous reedy ground. Actually the path was very reasonable as it wound its way to the higher ground beyond the first stile – I wondered whether we were being observed from the Windermre-Oxenholme train as it momentarily shared our terrain.

Damp crossing

The path now linked two small groups of trees via a pleasant ovine-grazed pasture before it passed through a gate to follow a defined cart track up to the picturesque property of Whasdike, which we passed, clockwise, out onto its access road.

From the cart track, the views northwards were enhanced by the areas of short-lived j e w e l l e d - s u n l i g h t between the shadowed ground and the dark stormy skies above. This situation occurred time and again over the next couple of hours.

Whasdike

Wetherlam

We followed the access road for a short distance, but as it turned sharp left we carried forward across another reedy field to enter the 'free-to-roam' area of School Knott Plantation. We eased upwards through thin birch woodland before shortly finding ourselves on open fellside.

Rainbow 2

Through the birches

Once out in the open we realized that the clouds had thickened once again, but as we were still in our unused waterproofs etc., we felt that we were ready for anything we might have to face. We resisted the temptation to turn left to tackle School Knott from this angle and proceeded to traverse around the upland until a distinct path was joined from the right. This move helped us enjoy the northern aspects 'neath the ensuing gloom.

School Knott

And out onto the open fell

At the junction, we turned left to start a reasonably steady ascent up the shoulder of School Knott. The obvious path soon gave way to several grassy alternatives as we neared the 760 foot cairnless summit. As with many of these low outlying fells the views offered were most rewarding.

From the top we headed down a fine grass path in the direction of a large tarn nestled rather nicely in a fold of the hills.

Windermere!

A jewel of sunlight

Rainbow 3

The Eastern Fells as we neared the top of School Knott

Grandsire beyond School Knott Tarn

As we passed through a gate to walk along the banks of the Tarn, we could see that it supported a family of swans busily foraging in the water and quite oblivious to our presence.

Admiring them, without disturbing them, we crossed the plank bridge over the run-off stream, clambered over the stile and scrambled up the slight banking to join a mature path from the right.

The family of swans

The path, like the one on School Knott, soon petered out, leaving us more or less to our own devices to attain the 815 foot cairned summit of Grandsire.

North across School Knott Tarn

Back to School Knott

The cairn was actually a solidly structured pile of stones; once again, the prospects were excellent. As the weather took on a more friendly turn we decided to camp down in the lee of the fell to enjoy a little respite and lunch.

School Knott and Windermere

Grandsire

Our perch overlooked the farmstead of Hag End, guarded, over a nearby wall, by a couple of very noisy geese who didn't care much for our presence – who needs guard dogs? Now, without much warning the skies had taken on a most ominous look, with heavy black clouds rolling in over the summit – it was time to be off! We had just made it down to Hag End when the heavens opened!! But, thank goodness, it was over and done with in a few minutes as we made a rather ridiculous effort to shelter under a few leafless sycamore trees at the farmstead. We were no worse for the soaking as we made our way down the farm's access drive to a narrow country lane. Here we turned right, but only for a short distance, because on arriving at the property known as Outrun Nook we turned left along a well-defined green path crossing verdant pastures.

From Outrun Nook in the sunshine

But still threatening skies

Through the gate, around a slight headland, over a wall and we were suddenly presented with a problem. Ahead of us the path crossed a flat marshy area for all the world like the bed of a drained-off tarn; however, because of all the recent rain, the 'drain-off' had had little effect! The path, until it disappeared underwater, appeared to be aiming for a peninsula of higher rocky ground. Carefully a scouting party of one ventured out into the saturated zone and, by using the clumps of reeds, negotiated a compromise path to the outcrop. All across! Phew! And we were quickly onto solid ground rising over a small mound to the group of buildings at Borwick Fold.

Problem?

Borwick Fold

Nearly straight across the lane (slightly right) we passed through a neglected area of the farmstead to follow the path by the side of a wall separating us from a wood. To our left, despite the changeable weather, we had excellent views of our pre-lunch conquest of Grandsire, but ahead of us, the weather looked grim. After following the wall for a short distance, we cut across the end of the wood to find that the path would lead us down through what looked like further saturated land. We refused the invitation but instead crossed a few yards to the right, which enabled us to access the comfort of solid tarmac beneath our feet.

By the wood

Grandsire

As we strode to the left down the lane, ahead of us the weather over the hills had changed once again, this time bedecked with sunshine. In the blink of an eye this changed – back to the heavy black clouds threatening to deposit their heavy load at any moment. We hurried on, covering the last mile back to the cars in double quick time.

Sunlit fells

'Nothing ventured, nothing gained' – and we'd had a good walk with great potential for future reference. Yes, I think that we will return. The walk was also ideal for Margaret's second outing after her broken arm ordeal some three weeks previously – still in her sling, she did really well.

N.B. By the 19th, parts of the Lakes, especially Cockermouth, were suffering from the most horrendous and destructive flooding to have been endured for a long time.

CHAPTER 9

CLAPHAM - CRUMMACKDALE

'PURE DELIGHT'

7 MILES

04 – 12 – 09

CLAPHAM - CRUMMACKDALE

7 MILES (NB MAP NOT TO SCALE)

04 – 12 – 09

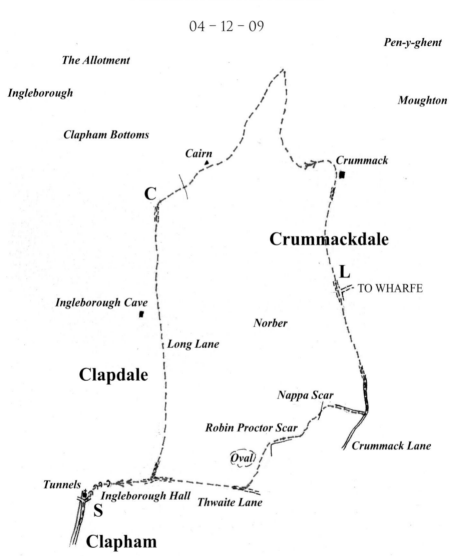

Pen-y-ghent

The Allotment

Ingleborough

Moughton

Clapham Bottoms

Cairn

Crummack

C

Crummackdale

L

TO WHARFE

Ingleborough Cave

Norber

Long Lane

Clapdale

Nappa Scar

Robin Proctor Scar

Oval

Crummack Lane

Tunnels

Ingleborough Hall   Thwaite Lane

S

Clapham

Map: Ordnance Survey Explorer OL2 – Yorkshire Dales – South and West

Start: GR 746694

Once again in this miserable early winter we hit the jackpot! It had been a terrible week, rain and wind, but this Friday we were hopeful for a change and looked for the window of good weather to manifest itself – and so it turned out; expanses of blue sky, clouds gently kissing the tops, a calmness which was hard to believe and a really warm wintry sun. Ideal for walking, especially in limestone country with guaranteed solid ground underfoot. The ten of us were eager to be off from a nearly deserted Clapham (usually a little honeypot); in fact we were able to park on the wide street adjacent to fast-flowing Clapham Beck.

From the cars, we followed the road up to the church to then turn right onto a solid but rough track (Thwaite Lane). Immediately we were passing through two extended tunnels to then commence a reasonable 'cardiovascular' climb which, to a few of us, proved to be rather hard work so early in the day. The tunnels were built by a previous owner of Ingleborough Hall so that they could have easier access to parts of their estate; also the drovers could pass through their estate without invading their privacy.

Thwaite Lane tunnel and 'cardio'

Long Lane

Eventually, as the lane finally levelled out, we stragglers caught the rest up at the junction with another rough track. We turned left into Long Lane, another walled drovers' road, leading northwards in the direction of Clapham Bottoms. After an initial steep descent, the next mile or so, above Clapdale on the left, was a steady climb, leading up to a gate which discharged us from the confines of the lane out onto the open fellside. We partook of coffee.

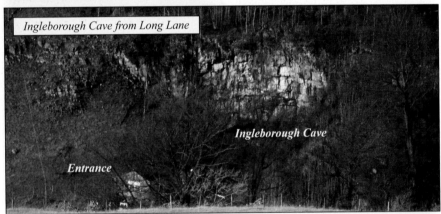

Ingleborough Cave from Long Lane

Ingleborough Cave

Entrance

The end of Long Lane

The Allotment

Clapham Bottom

Whilst enjoying coffee we looked down across the old mining area known as Clapham Bottoms to our left and upwards to The Allotment on the slopes of Simon Fell, an area riddled with well-known potholes. We now eased right and immediately started to enjoy the delights of walking in limestone territory. The green path rose gently to a stile, continuing forward towards a cairn on the skyline.

To the cairn

Ingleborough

The path levelled out, heightening our enjoyment along the high level green road, a well-used thoroughfare in years gone by, used by cattlemen heading for Selside and the Ribble Valley. To our left Ingleborough raised its flat top above the fleecy clouds whilst to the right Pen-y-ghent was the centre of attention.

Pen-y-ghent

We carried forward along the green track; I was now hoping that we would reacquaint ourselves with a most unusual sign. On our last walk along this path, at a junction we came across a regulation road sign set in a concrete bollard indicating 'NO ACCESS FOR CARS AND MOTORCYCLES' – most odd at such a high and remote location. It began to look as if the perpetrators had realized this as it had now vanished – we searched in vain. So we turned right and doubled back slightly on ourselves to follow the ridge in the direction of Norber. As the path eased down to the left we followed it into the beautiful valley of Crummackdale. From the flanks, we looked at Moughton Scars to the left, across to Moughton itself, and to the right, Smearset Scar and the low hills between Feizor and Stainforth.

Pen-y-ghent beyond Moughton Scars

Moughton

Smearset Scar

Crummackdale

Moughton

Norber

We soon found ourselves at the only habitation in Upper Crummackdale, that of Crummack. Turning right we rounded the farm and strode out along its solid access road, enjoying the valley's beauty so much so that I had quite forgotten about lunch until reminded in the most tactful manner!! 'Eh! When are we having dinner or are you out to beat P and V's time at Coniston?' So we dined at the junction of the walled track leading to the hamlet of Wharfe.

Views from
Crummackdale

Towards Wharfe

Moughton

Looking back to Upper Crummackdale

Refreshed and with less mutiny in the ranks, we pressed on along the access road until, just beyond the highest point (now Crummack Lane), we clambered up the right-hand banking to go over a stile onto a high level path by a wall to overlook a wide circular depression. The path narrowed as it passed below the quarry-like face of Nappa Scar and onto the lower slopes of Norber, boulders included.

The path narrows

Over the stone stile and through the boulders

Once over the high stone stile, the path wandered through the myriad of boulders until a fingerpost was reached, pointing up the gulley to the real Norber, strewn with its giant boulders (well worth a visit).

The path now dropped down to follow a wall beneath the vertical crags of Robin Proctor Scar. As the wall turned sharp left, the track eased right to pass by an unusual broken-walled oval area of what looked like marshy ground. Walled? Why? To keep animals out? Had it dried out in recent times (broken wall)? Interesting… all these speculations!

Robin Proctor Scar

The oval patch

We trekked across the green sward up to the stile leading us back onto Thwaite Lane. Despite the excellent weather of the day, the light was quickly reducing so we didn't waste too much time in turning right and heading back towards Clapham. What a relief to be going down this morning's ascent, through the now quite dark tunnels and out by the church, into the distinctly 'grey' Clapham.

We had had a fantastic day out on the fells and it was with a feeling of well-being and great satisfaction that we discarded our outer garments and headed back for Lancashire.

CHAPTER 10

WARTON CRAG

'TWICE!'

7 MILES

08 – 02 – 10

WARTON CRAG

7 MILES (NB MAP NOT TO SCALE)

08 – 02 – 10

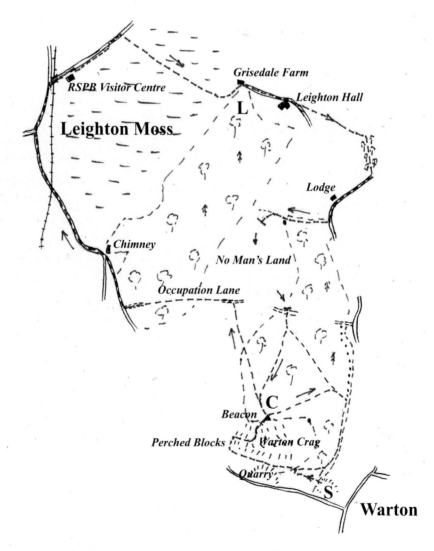

Map: Ordnance Survey Explorer OL 7 – The English Lakes South-Eastern Area
Start: GR 498724

And it finally came to pass that the great follower of the footpath – over hill and down dale, across swamp and through forest, over moorland and along the seashore, through rocky terrain and limestone pavements – on Monday 8th February, got his comeuppance!!! It became obvious that we were on the wrong path!! Though in my defence, you couldn't really say that we were lost, only slightly off track but still in familiar surroundings. And it had, up to that point, been such a good and satisfying day. But more of that later!

Nine of us and Poppy assembled on the small quarry car park, a hundred yards or so on the right along the narrow road by the side of the Washington pub in the village of Warton. We were soon making our way along the track which left the quarry at the back corner. This quickly turned into a 'cardiovascular' over uneven and quite slippery ground.

Out of the quarry

Early 'cardio'

After the customary recuperation stops, the last pull took us through a squeeze stile followed by a short awkward rise to a wooden kissing gate. From this point, we eased diagonally left to follow a track leading along a grassy terrace to soon look down onto the bottom of a large quarry, which was now used as a car park.

Perhaps at this point, especially if the reader is a potential walker, I should emphasize that Warton Crag is covered with a myriad of footpaths and that, with this in mind, there are many ways of attaining the summit and also of descending from the Crag. In reality, take your pick!![1] For our part, we continued along the terrace, enjoying the ever-developing views of the flat lowlands of the River Keer's estuary and beyond across Morecambe Bay to the dreadful, but necessary, towers of Heysham Power Station.

Along the first terrace

Southern aspects from the first terrace

Perched Blocks

As the terrace narrowed, we eased right up to the next one, ending up close to a group of huge rocks locally known as the Perched Blocks. From here, we headed westwards to immediately bear right through some bushes to then gain the top of another terrace, and turning right went forward to a major cross path. At this point, we turned left to clamber along a narrow cleft diagonally up a steep rock face.

Top of the cleft

The forlorn beacon

We were now within easy reach of the summit as the old rusty neglected beacon came into view – this spot is reputed to be the site of an 'Armada' beacon but the present incumbent was most probably due to either Jubilee or Millennium celebrations – it looked a sorry sight!! Within yards, the summit trig-point appeared and here we had coffee – hard work done!

Coffee time

Totally refreshed, we now headed north, easing left at the first junction, along a well-defined path, steadily downhill, through a very mossy but rather attractive landscape. This was quite a contrast to the grassy and exposed limestone of the morning's clamber on the scar face.

Mossy landscape

Open aspect

Occupation Lane

Shortly the track moved into a more open aspect as the silver birch numbers decreased, to be replaced by a bracken and fern environment. We soon joined a walled lane (Occupation Lane), an old drovers' road across the back of Warton Crag. With a left turn, this well-vegetated lane was followed down to the country lane from Warton. By bearing right, the main road was soon reached at Crag Foot, dominated by a high ivy-clad chimney, the remains of a pumping station for a land drainage scheme started in the early 19th century.

Main road junction

High chimney

Crag Foot

The western edge of Leighton Moss, an RSPB reserve, famous for its bitterns and of international importance, was viewed as we progressed along the main road (over a level crossing, right and right again at consecutive junctions) round to the reserve's Visitor Centre.

Across Leighton Moss

After a short comfort stop at the Centre, we followed the road for a few yards to then pass through a gate on our right onto a gravel path adjacent to the road. The path re-joined the road and then, after a further small yardage, we turned right onto a wide track taking us in a straight line across the marshland of the Reserve. Out along this solid path, we found ourselves more or less at water level; this was most noticeable as we passed the gaps that had been made in the high-standing autumnal reeds.

RSPB Visitor Centre

Across Leighton Moss

Leighton Moss

At water level

As the ground rose away from the edge of the Moss we found a few rocks amid some mole hills close to a well-supported barn to partake of a well-deserved lunch. Duly sustained we headed off, left, to the nearby Grisedale Farm where we joined a narrow tarmac road taking us to the precincts of Leighton Hall, a grey regal establishment belonging to the Gillow family of furniture fame.

Leighton Hall

As walkers, on reaching the entrance of Leighton Hall we were directed, in no uncertain terms, which way to go next – straight up the hill (a nasty piece of 'cardio') and NOT along the drive. Still, there were compensations: at each halt, which for me were rather frequent, the northern aspects developed as Grange-over-Sands and the Lakeland Fells came into our panoramic view.

The hill

Lakeland Fells

Grange

Leighton Moss

Leighton Hall

The Hill

Northern view

Once at the top (what a relief!), reunited with our patient colleagues, we turned right through the impressive beech trees along the top of the hill until we came to another narrow country lane – a right turn and we were soon down to the Lodge by the entrance to the Hall's driveway!! (See footnote 1 for alternative route from this point.)

Through the beeches

Just beyond a sharp left bend in the road we turned right along a path heading towards Crag Foot. A quarter-mile along this path we entered no-man's-land as we eased left to follow an obvious but, according to a damaged notice, unwelcoming track............

And so we reached Occupation Lane once again! Spot on!! At the designated place. I was really chuffed, internally preening myself with self-satisfaction. But oh, how the mighty are fallen!! Within minutes of re-entering the Warton Crag Nature Reserve I MISSED a path off to the left and before it was realized that a mistake had been made we were back on the track leading us back up to the 'BEACON'!! Whilst we weren't technically lost (just in the wrong place) it was rather embarrassing for me but terribly funny for everyone else – there will certainly be a decent mileage out of this situation – and why not? – everyone has a cross to bear!!

Anyway just before reaching the beacon (it could be seen) we turned left to follow a path downhill, sometimes dropping quite steeply over the limestone scars, until, after passing round a distinct hollow, we joined up with our intended path on the edge of the wood coating this side of the Crag.

On track – Occupation Lane!

Back on track! – a distant Ingleborough

So now we turned right, walking along the edge of the wood to eventually find ourselves at the kissing gate between the quarries which we had encountered in the first stages of our walk. Through the gate and an immediate left turn took us down the steep and often slippery path back to our cars nestled in the small quarry.

This was a great walk, with only a brief splattering of rain despite the covering of heavy and ominous clouds throughout the walk. It involved changing scenery, different exertions, a slight adventure into the unknown, but I've no doubt that this walk will always be remembered for that one lapsed moment of concentration!

———————————————

1. At this point walkers might feel happier carrying on down the road until the entrance to Occupation Lane is reached – a short walk will see you at our entrance point to the Nature Reserve. BUT don't miss that left turn! A nearly immediate left turn once into the Lane to follow the path along the edge of the wood could also be an alternative – there are plenty of paths to choose from!

ABOUT THE AUTHOR

John Singleton was born in June 1937 and, after his father's death in 1940, he was raised by his mother and her parents in Eccleston; a village on the edge of the West Lancashire Plain.

He attended Balshaw's Grammar School in Leyland and later Didsbury College in Manchester where he qualified as a teacher. His teaching career was at a local Comprehensive where, before retirement, he occupied the positions of Senior Teacher and Head of Science.

In April 1955, he met Margaret. They were married in 1959 and are still enjoying a great relationship. They have a family of three and five grandchildren.

For many years the family home was a two acre smallholding in Mawdesley where they all enjoyed 'a-good-life' style of living.

John enjoys numerous activities including sport, amateur dramatics, fell walking and being the secretary of the local agricultural society.

On thinking about his life, due to this short biography, he has realised just what a fruitful and interesting life he has experienced and also the number of people he should thank for this. Now, at this late stage of his life, he believes he has been given the opportunity to start a new career – one that he looks forward to.